The New Wisdom

The Esoteric of the New Age for Light-workers and Healers

Nic Kolbe

The New Wisdom: The Esoteric of the New Age for Light-workers and Healers.

Nic Kolbe has a diploma as a meditation teacher (U.S.A.) and is a certified professional spiritual healer (UK) and advanced QuantumTouch practitioner (U.S.A.). To learn more about Nic Kolbe's work, please contact him through his website: www.belight-healing.com

Library of Congress Cataloguing-in-Publication Data

Kolbe Nic

The New Wisdom: The Esoteric of the New Age for Light-workers and Healers.

ISBN: 9781513618791 Paperback
ISBN: 9781513618807 eBook

1. Spiritual 2. Personal Growth/General 3. Healing

First edition, (May 2017)

Cover Design by Sigi Kolbe, more info: www.sigi-kolbe.com

Empowered Whole Being Press
www.EmpoweredWholeBeingPress.com

Foreword

"Thank you, Nic Kolbe, for this valuable dissemination of one of the most compelling subjects of our time. I come away with the hopeful feeling of 'let there be light' for the future of humanity." Amber Wolf, PhD

ABOUT THE NEW WISDOM

This is the Esoteric teaching of the New Age for light-workers and healers. Light-workers are humans who are in ceremony, prayer, meditation, doing energy work as healer, or in any other form. They are compassionate to the person next to them. Healers are light-workers who provide an energetic platform to others for self-healing.

The essence of this information is the universal way of permanently switching on the inner Divine white light of the Creative Source by understanding that we are an extension of God.

After the shift of 2012, life for the light-worker and healer became about abundance and synchronicity, to awaken to multi-dimensionality and to activate full potentials in health and youth, in order to live a long and happy life without karma, drama, anger and fear.

The purpose of this information is to elevate human awareness of our majesty and abilities, to change the perception of the mind and to help create a great future for all. This teaching will always be subject to changes and additions, for everything is in motion and new tools become available as we move along, increasing our consciousness and cellular vibration.

The New Age is the age of information and light, and the emerging teachers of the New Age are aware of their interconnection and unity with the Higher Self.

When I began energy healing, I was made aware of the fact that my energy flow is extremely strong, as is the heat flowing out of my hands. Naturally, I was looking for explanations for myself and later for others, patients and fellow healers alike. I was aware at that time that years of meditation had made a difference in my cellular vibration, and later I understood more of the principles after listening to the Kryon channelings by Lee Carroll, as his teachings and affirmations create a new level of understanding.

Over time, people asked me to write down some of the principles of my practice, which I did. These turned out to be two sets of instructions, namely a basic one for light-workers and an additional one for healers. The instruction set for light-workers is the essence of the channelings of Kryon, whereas Part 2 — The Esoteric of the New Age for Healers — is based on principles I created during healing sessions with patients, and includes proven tools and techniques.

Love and light!
Nic Kolbe, January 2017

To my parents

I am that I am

ACKNOWLEDGEMENTS

I would like to thank the people who have given me invaluable assistance in my writing of The New Wisdom: in particular my wife Sigi for questioning everything; the great people at Empowered Whole Being Press, especially Candace Stuart-Findlay who went the extra mile to make this book a success; Beth Volz and Elaine-Martha Thompson for proofing the manuscript and Dr. Amber Wolf for the outstanding foreword.

TABLE OF CONTENTS

Part 1:

The Esoteric of the New Age for Light-workers

THE NEW AGE

Many things have been said and written about the New Age. Most of it is misconceived and simply not true, for it originated within the energy of the old, before the energetic shift of the planet in 2012. Because of this, people in some cultures have a bad association with the term "New Age" and some people even believe the "New Ager" to be evil.

Let us clear up the issue with an explanation based on the experience within the New Age. The New Age is the period of time after the energetic shift of 2012. The energetic shift is a galactic event that aligns our planet with the centre of the galaxy in a 36-year period of time at the end of a 26,000-year cycle, the precession of the Equinox. The exact value is 65 Mayan Baktun, which translates to 9,360,000 days or 25,626.81 years.

We moved into this energy 18 years before 2012 and will have this special energy fading out by 2030. To put all of it in a simple picture, one could say that until the end of 2012 the dark was pushing permanently upon us; in 2013 there was a balancing and since the beginning of 2014 the dark-light ratio on this planet has been changing dramatically. This is in favor of everybody working the puzzle of dark and light.

This was human civilization's fifth attempt to develop from a zero point and to make the shift happen. Four times civilization as such destroyed itself in the past on this planet. Five is the number of change in Tibetan Numerology and this time we did not destroy ourselves but rather decided to upgrade our vibration.

Humanity became aware of the interplay between dark and light more than 50,000 years ago; the Mayans knew about it and kept a calendar of consciousness, which ran out of time on December 12, 2012. Each dispensation of consciousness had a timeframe of about 10,000 years. Our age started approximately 5125 years ago and ended with the precession of the Equinox in 2012.

The universe is more willing than ever to provide synchronicity and beautiful solutions to all problems, if humans choose to open themselves up to it. Light-workers can step out of their protective shell, open up to abundance and be accepted in their community for what they are. There is no reason to be considered weird anymore.

This is the beginning of the age of enlightenment on this planet and some humans will make the best of it, creating beautiful lives for themselves and others, filled with compassion, love and joy.

In the process, light-workers plant the seeds of light and claim their divinity within themselves. The plants will grow slowly and it will take a few generations to see dramatic change in consciousness, with new children being born every day and old energy passing away.

This is the true meaning of the New Age. It is the time that many have been trained for in so many lifetimes, to lead the way with joy, even if the media only shows bad news and people around us tremble and spin in drama, anger and fear. The secret is, to create our own bubble of reality.

The New Age is the time to claim the mastery within and to use an incredible set of new tools that help create a better connection to the Creative Source. Everything changes slowly, and I like to picture it as the moving of Earth through a portal in space – anything that is not based on compassion and integrity will not pass through it. Welcome to the age of a new consciousness of humanity.

"All you need is love" is not entirely true anymore. Before the shift of 2012, the highest energy available for light-workers was love and it still is the basis of most healing methods available today. Due to the shift, most light-workers are now able to use the next higher energetic level of compassion, which is supported by the increased consciousness of humanity and energy of the planet.

Love leads to compassion! As it happens with love, there are also several layers of compassion, starting with the compassion towards one self, then towards others and then moving into the final state of unconditional compassion. This is based on the realization that there is no difference between others and us, since we all are pieces of the Creator playing our part in this dimension.

The energetic numeric value of compassion is 33 and corresponds very much with the percentage of DNA activated by most humans at this moment. For most light-workers in the New Age, the expression of compassion will bring amazing new results within the field with which they are working.

However, there are exceptions. Very old souls, who have re-calibrated early and have already moved into the next activation level of 44 percent of DNA, are much more connected to the source. Because of their close connection to the source, they also experience the overwhelming joy of it and are able to reflect that ultimate joy into their light work. These are, at the moment, the master healers and teachers of the teachers, the ones who can hold more light.

Compassion leads to joy! One of the next higher numeric values of energy (44-99) is "Joy of the Creator" and humans with that connective experience can use this energy to its fullest when working the light. This will be the next standard for all humans within a few lifetimes and the norm for healers from the next life on or maybe already now? It all depends on you…how much you want it and how pure your intent is.

I have been teaching this for years, the principle of how to increase the flow of light through love, compassion and joy.

Light-worker wake up! This is not grade one anymore and it is not new information that everything is love, including to love yourself. That's just the basics! Now for the graduation: enhance the communication with the Spirit through the training of intuitive thought by using the pineal gland. The frontal exit point of the pineal gland is known as the third-eye chakra and you can find exercises of activation at the end of the book.

The way we treat others is the measure of activation of our God-part within, and since all the answers are found within, you do not need another teacher.

How are we doing today? Fair…if we consider that the average intellect and spiritual awareness of humans at this point is placed around three in a scale of ten, give or take two points up or down for certain individuals. Here is what comes next: The upcoming years within the shift have a very special energy, to increase our abilities much more than any other time in human history or the future.

You may gain two or three points within this very short time when working the puzzle with intent and purity. Furthermore, our solar system recently entered a place in space with a different energy, which will increase the level of awareness of all humanity by one point.

Let us do some mathematics: The light-workers and healers who have re-calibrated to the new energy of the shift are around four, and will gain an average of two more for the effort, and one more for free (because of the solar system moving into a new energy), which add up to seven.

Do you realize that all the masters from all the scriptures had around eight and you can reach six or more within this short time? I find that truly amazing! Yes, the numbers also reflect the activation of your DNA where 10 equals 100 percent. Better get on with it! It's time to drop all the spiritual nonsense and cosmetics that confuse so many and stop cruising along in this New Age movement. If you have not re-calibrated yet and are still battling with anger, drama and fear, then it is high time to drop them! You are a master; now 'Claim your mastery'.

THE SPLIT AT BIRTH

Before humans are born, they are fully developed beings in a physical sense, but it is only at the moment of birth that the energy of the planet is measured. The functionality of the DNA adjusts itself to that percentage and the soul attaches itself permanently to the body until departure.

There is no linearity in multi-dimensionality. As a human with a linear consciousness you perceive a 3- or 4-dimensional world, depending on which view you prefer. This is the playground of humanity for using free will in a reality described by the velocity of the speed of Light, Gravity and Magnetism, plus the weak and strong Quantum forces that scientists still need to discover and understand.

By November 2015, scientists found evidence of an immediate response of entangled electrons over a far distance, not limited to the speed of light. These higher, all-including dimensional worlds are higher in vibration. All is in the now and all is connected to the Source and aware of it at all times. When we are home, we have the mind of God and are fully aware that we are a piece of the Creator.

It is difficult to describe "we" and separate us from other beings of creation, but to put it in the most accurate way: We are special! We belong to a most powerful soul group that is working the multi-dimensional puzzle of creation in one of its lower vibrating domains: this visible universe.

We are assigned to the only planet of free choice regarding light and dark in this galaxy and when we take the step into this world, most remember absolutely nothing about anything whatsoever. We have planned everything well in advance, which includes all the souls involved in our process of growth and discovery — our family, friends and enemies.

We have played this puzzle before on other Earth-like planets and there are civilizations in the galaxy many millions of years old. At the moment, Earth is very attractive to newcomers from many different star systems.

When we come in into this body at birth, only a small part of us enters, since our full soul cannot be contained in a physical body with only about 30 percent of the DNA activated. If the full soul did come in, the physical body would simply explode and create quite a lightshow. That means that a part of our soul remains in the multi-dimensionality of God.

The soul-part that attaches itself to our body, the Higher Self, whilst fully connected to the other side, splits up into Higher Self, guides, a 'Spiritual Entourage' and your Innate (on the inside from a 3-D point of view to be explained later). Part of the expression of the Higher Self in 3-D is our consciousness, the part that we think we are. Here are three energies (on the outside from a 3-D point of view) we can work with, which make up our first team:

The Higher Self is our connection to the 'other side' through our soul. As we later see, the Higher Self is also woven into the fabric of the physical body, right into the DNA. This is why we want to have a permanent meld between consciousness and Higher Self, to be able to switch on the inner light.

A good affirmation would be: "Dear Higher Self, I love you! I give pure intent for a complete meld with my consciousness. Please help me in all things and to be more light!"

Your guides are multi-dimensional parts of you that will look ahead in time, so to speak. They know what the largest energetic potentials are of something to happen in your reality. A good affirmation would be: "Dear guides, thank you and I love you! Please guide me, I trust your guidance."

Your Spiritual Entourage comprises part of you and part others, that attach parts of themselves to you for your growth, guidance and protection. All loved ones, who have left this realm before you, are attached to your entourage. Our Higher Self and the Entourage are also 'in charge' of making synchronicities happen, since our soul parts 'on the other side' plan potentials to happen with the soul parts of other human beings right next to us. A good affirmation would be: "Dear Spiritual Entourage, thank you and I love you! Please make the synchronicities happen to put me at the right place at the right time, to meet the right people, who have solutions to my problems." I would call that the 'sweet spot'.

The one cosmic law Spirit has to obey is the free will of humans to decide if they want to move towards the light or dark. These entities are always with you, but can only touch you with your permission. Know your team and expect synchronicities! Synchronicities are energies aligned with purpose that look like accidents.

APPRECIATE THE SITUATION

Sometimes you find yourself in a situation, be it at work or home, that you don't want to be in at all and you pray every day: "Dear God, please remove me from this place, why do I have to endure this? Anything else would be better! Everything is dark and there is nothing positive." You find yourself in a place that is dark and you do not understand that you might be the only one to shine some light right there. Since you are still in karma, you have ended up in that situation by your own doing. By switching on your light in that situation you change everything – you also solve your karmatic imprint, which is the energy you brought into this life from previous incarnations.

Many find themselves in very dark places because that is where the most light is needed! What happens if you shine your light of love, compassion and joy into a dark situation? People can now see the ugly things that were in the dark before and because of it they will make different decisions. Because of your light, the intuitive sight of others gets better and suddenly new dynamics will present themselves and a hopeless dark situation becomes joyful and pleasant. Understand this: You are the only one who can handle the situation and effect a win-win solution.

There are many more entities of light in the universe, such as angels*, masters, helpers and others, all with different qualities, powers and properties of the light that can be invoked to help. These are separate entities in the 'soup of creation', other teams you might want to work with, but they are not included in this teaching. This teaching is about the multi-dimensional parts of you and how to enhance your own creative power.

The most important factor to be aware of is that before the split we are a magnificent piece of God and we can realize it by connecting the consciousness to the Higher Self! A good affirmation would be: "Glory to the Creator, for I am a magnificent piece of God!" Understand: You truly are a magnificent piece of God.

* There is a basic explanation, for the purpose of daily affirmations, of angels in a later chapter, since they play such an important part with humans.

WHO ARE YOU?

There are different soul groups on this planet from all over the galaxy, but generally we can group them into three classifications. This has to do with the information we can access from previous lives on this planet, which has been called the "Akashic Record":

The newcomer souls: Most souls on the planet at this point in time are in this group, which also explains the population growth on Earth and where these 'new' souls come from, namely from all over the galaxy. The newcomers are easily fooled because they have no information from previous lifetimes on this planet and are therefore clueless. Nevertheless, some of them are from the outset instantly drawn to the light – and in the process bring forward qualities they earned in past lives on another planet.

The intermediate souls: Many of the souls on Earth belong to this group, with a few hundreds of years of experience on this planet. All they ever experienced on Earth were the Dark Ages, which is why there is so much negativity and darkness in them. These souls like to experience the Creator through spiritual boxes with rules and regulations, putting human qualities and attributes on divinity. Valuable lessons are stored in the Akashic Record but are not integrated, since karma is the trigger of action.

The old souls: This soul group has been incarnating on this planet for more than 1,000 lifetimes and its members have experienced everything possible on this planet. A treasure of wisdom and information is stored in the Akashic Record and most of them are awakening to it. This group is only about half a percent of the population and not all of them are awakening in this lifetime.

Some of this group even go more than 50,000 years back and are from the original seeding group in Lemuria, a select group of old souls on this planet, who are ancient galactic light-workers. The old souls are not an elite group, but they are more experienced, having the gift of remembrance of the Akashic Records and therefore the wisdom of the Ages.

If you are reading this, you are most likely an old soul, otherwise you would not be interested in it in the first place. The old souls are awakening first: they are drawn to the light and no spiritual box will match their magnificence. Only the truth of the Creator inside is the aim.

You are a specialist of Paradigm Change, the first to get started when the population of a planet decides to move towards the light and to increase the level of consciousness. The task is, with free choice, to switch on the light, to plant and water the seeds of light through love, compassion and joy.

It is a difficult task, but it has never been easier, since for the first time the energy of the planet supports more light. You are well prepared, some of you through millennia of lifetimes on this planet, in any possible scenarios. You are highly trained specialists with amazing new tools, most of which were only available to a few masters in the past. Claim the new tools and be the light.

Coming next for humanity is an increased maturity of thinking in terms of seeing the potential future outcome of any action. This can be better understood by looking at a chess master who plans five moves ahead. One can also suggest the comparison that humanity at the moment sees in black and white, but is moving into seeing shades of grey – and only a few are able to perceive color.

Now is the beginning of a spiritual ascension on this planet, with the old souls understanding it first and then teaching it to others.

But you are not just an old soul – go beyond that; you are a piece of God. You are part of the Creative Source, which has no beginning and no end. A circle of reality that always was and always will be. There is only one truth in the universe: God exists!

All that is are imaginations and shades of the existence of God. All around you, all you can see is God's creation. Everywhere you look, with eyes that were created by God, you see God. God is looking at God through God.

As a human being you have free choice and a brain to question and figure it out. Understand: You are one of a team of the best-trained specialists for this job in the galaxy.

WHAT DID THE ANCIENTS KNOW?

The first thing the ancients did when going into ceremony was to honor Gaia the Earth, and second, to honor the ancestors.

Honor Gaia for the love and support, which is essential for everything on the planet. The truth is, there is a chain of support. The sun receives energy and information from the centre of our galaxy. The sun supports the Earth and the Earth supports humans. Another reason to honor Gaia is the new energy on the planet; this will also show your understanding of the shift and the Divine plan.

Honor the ancestors for their love and wisdom. The shamans of South America still connect to their ancestors when looking for guidance. Another reason to honor the ancestors is that if you have been on this planet for several thousand lifetimes then you should have the understanding that you have been your own ancestors, too. This way you will honor yourself and the grandness of the Divine plan.

As a piece of the Creator, you have watched the birth of this universe and yet, here you are in a physical body and worry about money.

COMPREHEND TIME

Time is an abstract and added to the 3-D world, and is used to describe a specific moment in the fabric of the 3-D space-time. Time works in repeated circles and different layers of circles within circles. Nature is filled with circles in time, in the water, the solar flares, the moon phases, the revolutions around the galactic centre, etc.

With the implementation of the increasing energy, we not only look at circles but at spirals! The energetic markers in time have been coined "Time Fractals" by the great scientist Gregg Braden. They indicate an event and present themselves again and again in a circle with increased energetic potentials. We basically meet an old situation and with the increased energy we are given the opportunity to make better decisions. We can change the memory of how we react to the event!

This is also the explanation of prophecy, for Spirit can see the energetic markers in time and the strongest future potentials, depending on the global human consciousness at that moment in time.

Time is only in 3-D, otherwise everything else is 'being in the moment'. The illusion of time, the zero remembrance at birth and the free will of humans were necessary for the energetic test of humanity until the shift. Since humanity passed the marker of 2012 and chose to move into a higher consciousness, humans will remember more information about past lives at birth or young age.

You are eternal! The soul was never created, it always was. It never goes away, it always is – it has no beginning and no end!

THE NINE ENERGIES OF THE HUMAN

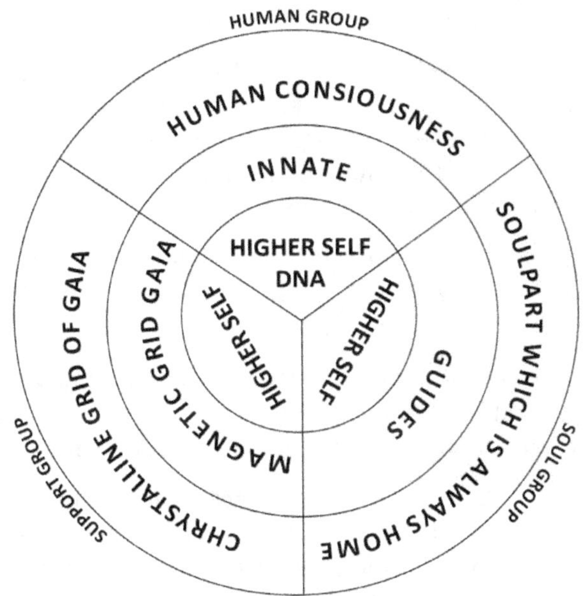

The number of energies within the human is complete, for the numerological energetic value of nine in Tibetan Numerology is completion. The explanation is the definition of the human of today, right after the shift. This definition will change over time, for humans are evolving.

The Creative Source does not put itself on the planet as the Creative Source, it splits apart. When you come into the planet only a portion of your soul arrives here, the portion that can be sustained in a corporeal body.

THE HUMAN GROUP

The human in its physicality consists of three energetic parts, which should be working closely together as one.

The *Higher Self* is the core Creative Source, the part of our 'Godliness', which is interwoven into our physical body. It vibrates at a higher level, which is why we call it Higher Self. It sits right in the multi-dimensional parts of each piece of DNA. Each cell of our body is vibrating in Spirit.

The *human consciousness* is what we identify ourselves with; it's who and what we think we are. It's the part that makes the decision about what we do next.

The *innate body intelligence* is that part in our body that knows everything about the body but nothing about the outside, since it is not fully connected to Higher Self or consciousness.

The Innate is that what we are using when practicing Kinesiology/muscle-testing, working with pendulums or tarot cards, to find answers about sickness inside the body, allergies or best diet. It is the body bridge between consciousness and Higher Self, most important and still something we hardly know about. Innate is the intelligence of DNA.

A good affirmation would be: "Dear Innate, dear Higher Self, I love you! I give pure intent for a complete meld of my consciousness with Innate and Higher Self. I am light!"

THE SOUL GROUP

The human in its spirituality consists of three energetic parts, which can be understood as:

The *Higher Self* again, is also part of the soul group. It's in all three groups, which shows how important the Higher Self is.

The *guides* of a human are truly multi-dimensional parts of the human, which are separated from the Higher Self to advise the human.

The *soul* part, which is always home, is in communication with the soul parts of other humans to bring forward synchronicity. Synchronicity is a term for when you are at the right situation at the right place and time.

A good affirmation would be: "Dear Higher Self, dear guides and dear soul – I love you. I am light!"

THE SUPPORT GROUP

The support group consists of three energetic parts, which are difficult to explain:

The *Higher Self* again, is also part of the support group. It's the three in one, the one in three.

The *Magnetic Grid of Gaia* is directly linked to the consciousness of humanity. The weaker the magnetism, the stronger is consciousness.

The *Crystalline Grid of Gaia* is the storage device of human emotions. The more light we create the more goes into the grid.

A good affirmation would be: "I am walking with the light of the Creator!" Understand: God is inside of you and you are God.

KARMA, VOWS AND LIFE LESSONS

Karma, vows and life lessons are three major energies, which worked well in the past and will work in the future for all who do not switch on the light and recognize the Creator within.

All three are meant to teach us by bringing forward energies into our current life. Without them humans would not evolve at all.

KARMA: The principle of karma has been studied well by the Hindus and is a major pillar in their philosophy. Karma is unsolved energetic puzzles from previous lives. Karma creates energetic triggers in time that push and pull you into a certain direction to give you an opportunity to act – or not to act, as the case may be.

VOWS: Many Vows have been given in past lives: to God, a Saint, a cause or a person. A typical example is the knight that vows to never love anybody other than Mother Mary, which might lead to problems of expression of love in this life.

LIFE LESSONS: Every lifetime has general Life Lessons, when coming in. A valid Life Lesson is to find happiness in family, another would be to experience and understand the early loss of a child.

All these energies are valid, since they have the aim to help us to find the Creator inside in this lifetime! Nevertheless, the awakening soul on this ascending planet has no use for these tools anymore and needs to switch them off. Free yourself from the old program and overwrite it with new information. A new vow could be: "I vow to be the light."

A good affirmation would be: "Dear Higher Self, dear Spirit, dear God, I give the pure intent to switch off karma, vows and life lessons, for they do not suit my magnificence anymore. I am light and want to touch the face of the Creator inside!"

STOP THE EGO

Ego stands in the way of everything! Ego puts one into the foreground and is pushy. If you have self-worth and self-confidence, ego is not needed anymore. Since by now you know who you are, switch off the ego. Ego stands in the way of love, compassion and light.

A very good exercise is to NOT talk about yourself unless asked! As affirmation you could use: "Dear Higher Self, please switch off my ego – I want to be in control of my ego, I am light."

THE INTENT

Pure intent is all that matters and is best explained with an anecdote of a person jumping into a pool of water. When you jump, you know you are getting wet! You prepare for it, and maybe even choose to attempt an impressive dive. It would be silly to jump and then try to fight gravity whilst falling.

Pure intent in spiritual things goes much deeper! Strong intent is something you want with all your heart and being, more than anything you've ever wanted before. It is a yearning deep down in the soul that grows stronger by the day. How far do you want to go? How much do you want it? Purity is when we have the intent without any involvement of the ego. To speak an affirmation with pure intent, you should be in a meditative state, for example keep your mind fixed on the third-eye chakra (between your eyebrows) when speaking the affirmation – otherwise one might not have the results hoped for. Your intent is the catalyst for the consciousness shift available to you.

Intent is combined with your creative power as the planting of seed or putting it forth. Then Spirit will take care of it to make it work. The more you are aware that you have the powers of the Creator, the better the results. This will also be enhanced by a great amount of training! Every new power needs to be trained, and what seems to be impossible at the beginning will be something routine later.

THE ANGELS

Angels do exist! They work together in support of humans, e.g., at birth, when passing over, and if we allow it, in many ways during a human life. For instance, they are in the hospital to support when one is having surgery, and they are also with the energy healer when they pour light into the patient.

There is no hierarchy within the angels. Even archangels are not a singular entity, but rather a group energy that is different every time and which is part of the 'angel-soup', a part of the whole 'Creative Soup'. At times, some seem to be more important than others, but that is only a human perception.

Angels look different to every human, since they usually show themselves in a way that is comfortable to the human's box of beliefs, e.g. with wings or halos. If they were to show themselves in their original form as a radiant ball of light and too bright to look into, most humans would be afraid. That is the reason why when angels appeared to humans in the Holy Scriptures, the first thing they said was: "Do not be afraid!" That said, there is no bad angel that has fallen from grace and is now out to get your soul! That is absolute nonsense and a humanization of God, created by humans to put fear into other humans in order to control them.

There is only one rule about how to interact with angels: free choice on the part of humans. Angels are only allowed to interact with us, if we want it and ask for it!

Do angels become humans and vice-versa? No! Angels and humans are different groups in the soup of creation with different tasks. Humans do not become angels and angels do not incarnate as humans.

There are some beings from other stars on this planet, from societies that have spent more than a million years in an enlightened state. They have a body, but are mostly multi-dimensional. It will be difficult for us to differentiate between these beings and angels.

There is a lot of mythology around, especially with light-
workers. Use your spiritual logic to see the truth!

THE PINEAL GLAND

Whatever information you are able to receive from the higher dimension - from angels, guides or Spirit - is pushed via the pineal gland to the brain and the brain tries to make sense of it in a linear way.

The pineal gland is the centre of the third-eye and true Yogis are very familiar with it. Meditation in its essence is a process to enhance the connection through the pineal gland with intent and breathing. Also, some advanced spiritual healers are able to assist in opening the third-eye chakra and the crown chakra for a better connection to the Creative Source.

The pineal gland is the center of communication and is blocked or 'calcified' in most humans, mostly due to incorrect diet and lifestyle choices.

How does Spirit communicate through the pineal gland? The information provided by Spirit is non-linear, meaning all at once. It is that moment where you totally grasp a new concept in its finest detail, but find it later difficult to remember it when trying to analyze or to share it.

The concept of spiritual communication from Spirit to human is non-linear, whilst humans are linear. If the human allows for it and has trained his muscle of communication – the pineal gland – removes all the filters and asks the Spirit to speak up, to repeat the non-linear information and slow it down until it can be fully grasped. This is the advanced listening of spiritual communication.

Spiritual communication can also occur between humans, or humans and their pets, with the sending and receiving of concepts and visualizations in a non-linear way. As is the case so often, regular practice is the secret to successful spiritual communication.

QUANTUM DNA

Human DNA is special because it is unique to each human. Furthermore, all of the 100 trillion pieces of DNA inside a human are identical. All those pieces are connected to each other and act as one due to their magnetic fields overlapping, creating an effect known as magnetic induction. Therefore, DNA should be seen as one, for it is in an entangled state with itself!

The biggest part of us is not in 3-D, since only a small part of the soul can live in a human being who has activated approximately 33 percent of their DNA. Activating the DNA is the task and the secret to unlock new powers, which I will explain in the next chapters.

Science tries hard to understand the pieces of DNA in 3-D. Only recently it has been discovered that 95 percent of the non-protein-encoding parts are not junk. What really sits in the DNA is information and bookmarks of information that point to external sources, like the Chamber of Creation within Gaia.

Some of the aspects of DNA are comparable in modern terms with our access of information using a computer. Few parts are stored on the machine, for most information is acquired from the global network and 'cloud'.

Advancement in DNA is not happening in the chemical part of the DNA, for the chemistry is complete – the multi-dimensional parts of the DNA are activating. Since 2014, the energy of the planet has been supporting an activation of the DNA, depending on the free will and pure intent of humans.

Each piece of DNA contains a piece of the Creator; we are truly magnificent! The energetic field of the DNA radiates nearly nine meters from the human in all directions and has been named Merkabah (Hebrew "Mer" means light, "Ka" means Spirit and "Ba" means body, also vehicle of light or chariot).

The 2015 Nobel Prize for chemistry was awarded to Tomas Lindahl, Paul Modrich and Aziz Sancar, for the discovery of how the DNA repairs itself. In much earlier experiments, the Russian scientist Vladimir Poponin showed in his paper "The DNA Phantom Effect" that DNA influences light.

THE OPEN DOORS OF DNA

Before we start the teaching about DNA, I need to remind you that this is an attempt at bringing structure into something that is not linear.

We look at our DNA, but not in the scientific way of the double helix, molecules and atoms. Instead, we will use the analogy of a house, which we enter at one point and once inside, find a room with many doors.

Looking at the doors, we realize that most doors are closed – only three doors are open at this moment (2017). This is to show you that DNA, in itself, is complete but not fully functional.

CHEMICAL HEREDITY: This first door is wide open and it is the most basic principle of inheritance. Here you find the things you immediately recognize, namely the color of the eyes, the type of the body or the talent that was inherited from the parents. This is one of the major ways for information to be passed on within lineages of life forms, and this door will always be open.

IMMEDIATE AKASHIC INHERITANCE: The next door will always be open for all souls – except newcomers – and is the other important way for the universe to provide you with information from the past. This shows itself as creative passion that comes forward in a child and the parents have no idea where it comes from, for it is not in their genetic lineage. This is also the information that the past-life reader can access, with the energetic markers in the soup of information.

KARMA: This door has always been open, and in the room are found unfulfilled energetic puzzles. Karma creates energetic triggers in time, that push and pull you into a certain direction to give you opportunity to act – or not. Step out of karma in order to work the light; karma is not needed for an advanced old soul. Close the door of karma and steer your boat across the river of time with the purpose of a light-worker.

These are the basic elements of DNA that define humanity at this moment in time.

THE NEXT DOORS OF DNA

The following doors are closed and will open slowly for humanity after 2014; however, some of you have already opened some of these doors. It has to be that way, for you will be the examples and leaders in the future who know how to work the DNA.

INNATE: When this door opens, we have a body bridge between the Consciousness and the Higher Self. When you come closer to the innate intelligence of the body, several things manifest. One is the ability to look inside the physical body without external help: with the door closed you might develop a hidden sickness for a long time before a doctor will do tests and give you the diagnosis. Another way would be to go to a medical intuitive – who uses his/her Higher Self to look at your Innate. Also, you can go to a practitioner of Kinesiology or 'muscle-testing,' who will draw answers from your Innate.

With this door open, you will immediately know if there is something wrong in your body – you become your own medical intuitive. It is even more complex than this, since when Innate is more active, there is a stronger meld with the Higher Self.

The Innate will communicate with your DNA and to you (your consciousness) about your appropriate diet, to achieve a level of health unknown to humanity for many thousands of years. It will create a system of health in your body, immune to all disease and aging will be much slower.

SELF-BALANCE: With this door open, no matter how our energy might fluctuate, we quickly come back to balance. This refers to the usual daily changes, including regular upgrades to higher vibrations with the ongoing planetary change. This door will help you to find the middle and center back into balance.

WISDOM: Old soul, this door opens a whole room of treasures, which is the information of all our past lives on Earth stored in the Akashic record. Opening this door will also make you realize that you are your own ancestors, for you know you have been here before many times.

These are the basic doors of DNA. You have locked one and now there are five open. Five is the number of change in Tibetan Numerology. Everything is going to change when unlocking one or more of the doors.

THE DOORS OF ASCENSION

The next doors of DNA will open slowly, maybe in the next 10 years for humanity. These doors are difficult to open for a light-worker and it all depends on how much you want it!

NEVER ALONE: With this door open, you realize that you are not alone. You understand that you are multiple beings of light and one soul exists at several places at the same time – one of them being on the other side of our dimensionality.

No matter what happens at a certain moment in your life, you are not alone! The family around you is here and you can feel the loved ones that passed before, for they attach themselves as part of your spiritual entourage and guide-set – this also includes ancestors, removed in time.

They are with you to love and guide you and no matter what terms you were on with them at the moment of their departure, they are now fully aware about you and your amazing task. They are in awe that you made it, despite everything! You are truly never alone, ever!

COMPLETION OF PURPOSE: When this door opens, no matter what happens in your life, it is well with your soul. You see life as an extension of the Akash, fully understanding past and future lives.

There is no worry about how old you are right now and how long you will live in this lifetime. You see your life as multiples, a single soul changing suit every lifetime to have a fresh tool for working the light according to the energies at hand.

NO BIAS: This is a difficult door for the human, for we are born into a box of beliefs, a system that puts structure into how to interact with God and rules about what is appropriate in terms of worshipping God, and what is not. In order to open this door, we have to remove everything we have ever learned and use our spiritual logic to step out of the box of humanizing God.

Evaluate God and ask the question: "Dear God who are you? Who am I? Please bring forward what I need to know, is everything the way I was told, or is it different?" Before you can see God as a piece of everything you need to re-evaluate everything from a spiritual zero point and overwrite in your brain what is real and what is not – an unbiased view of all that is. It's all about YOU.

ANCIENT REMEMBRANCE: This door opens the qualities from a long past time at the beginning in Lemuria, when your DNA was activated to more than 50 percent. Since then we had a drastic drop even down to 20 percent in the Dark Ages and are now at a level of 33 percent. The activation of DNA is linked with the development of human consciousness as a whole.

There was no technology back then in a modern sense, but you had more knowledge about the Creator, yourself and simply everything.

When this door opens slowly, you will see the Akash and with it the wisdom of all things that you experienced will come through. You are your own ancestors! This creates a state of quiet wisdom where you don't have to prove anything to anybody.

STEM-CELL BLUEPRINT: The door of Stem-cell Blueprint will slowly open for some and it will be controversial. Other humans will see when you open this door because you will be healthier and your aging will be slower. At this moment, the system creates new cells in the body from copies and over time the copies show wear and tear. If nothing changes, that is the normal way the body works with decay, sickness, disease and age.

When going back to the original blueprint of the cells, which is stored in the DNA since birth, one can bring back health and live much longer in a younger body. "Dear DNA, dear Spirit, dear cellular structure, use the original blueprint when making new cells."

ACTIVATE QUALITIES FROM PAST LIVES

The storehouse of DNA for the 'Old Soul' is filled with many things and sometimes we want something specific to come forward into our current reality. This works well when wanting to become a better artist, poet or writer. We can also bring forward other information of previous life times, like the warrior or the healer. "Dear DNA, dear cellular structure, dear Spirit, please bring forward the healer".

There are many lifetimes as healer, monk, priest, shaman, etc. and many times we came close to the light – so tap into it! "Bring forward youth, health and wisdom" is a great general invocation.

The best way to get started, before making up the mind, what we think we need, would be to ask for what is best for us: "Dear DNA, dear cellular structure, dear Spirit, please bring forward what I need to know and not anything that does not suit my purpose". That way, we give Spirit a chance to put information on us that we need right now and also have an 'akashic filtering' against past life trauma coming up in our life and dreams.

THE GURU PRINCIPLE

For the last thousands of years, the Guru principle was the only way of reflecting the light in a lifetime. The dark energy of the past created a reality in which we struggled to survive, never mind reflecting the light.

Because of this, enlightened humans started to sequester themselves in places that are hard to reach, in caves and mountains, away from any civilization. Even today, there are enlightened beings on this planet, to balance and hold the light.

In the past, the Guru (outside) was the only way to gain access to the other side, but since the energetic shift we are able to access the other side by activating the Guru within. This is new and was not possible in the Dark Ages of the past, but in the age of illumination we activate our 'God part' right inside, which knows everything!

The ascending old soul cannot be satisfied anymore with any external guidance or Guru-ship, but will connect to the Guru inside. This information will not go down well with all the spiritual organizations, that insist on the hierarchy of priesthood and guru and the exclusivity of their mission. There is no need to point it out to them either, since for many humans that old way of connecting to God is still valid and blessed by God.

Blessed is the human being looking for the Creator in any way! Remember: Your belief enhances the truth that you carry.

SWITCH ON THE HEAT

There is a new energy around, which many light-workers are still confused about, as they are not achieving the results that they are looking for. In fact, it seems that it is getting more difficult to achieve the same level of vibration maintained before the shift.

Many light workers are drawn to new modalities and techniques, which at the end do not really increase the vibration of the body and this might create doubt and uncertainty within them.

In the new energy, all these modalities and techniques will not really work, unless you switch on your heat.

How to do this? Here are the two essential steps:

Love yourself and truly recognize that you are part of the Creator.

Love any other person who comes into your life and truly recognize that they are also a part of the Creator (even if they are not aware of it).

It's the basic Namaste-principle in its essence! The God in me greets the God in you. First, you need to recognize the God in yourself. Secondly, what do you see when you meet another? See the light in others first!

Only this will switch on your heat and bring out the power of all modalities and techniques you learned in this and past lifetimes. People will start to remark on the strong heat emanating from your hands and body; some might even see your strong light.

MONEY MATTERS

There are misconceptions about money. In the past energy, before the shift, it was appropriate for the light-worker to be poor and isolated from the world. In fact, it was seen as one of the requirements for connecting to the Spirit. This has been imprinted into our spiritual inheritance over many lifetimes.

In the new energy, this is not the proper action anymore! We are not here to suffer and there is an unlimited supply of support from the universe. People will not follow your light if you don't have abundance in your life!

The proper mindset will attract abundance! We are not only talking about money, but everything. One has to get out of survival mode to be able to shine more light.

Do not be stuck on "money will come my way" but rather use a daily affirmation like: "My life is filled with abundance and I am supported by the universe! I trust in the workings of Spirit."

If one is in tune with the Spirit, there can be no more worries about money and other 3-D things.

A good affirmation would be: "I am healthy, I am wealthy, I am in abundance of all things, great things are coming my way!"

STOP DRAMA, ANGER AND FEAR

As long as drama, anger and fear exist in our lives, the light cannot be switched on!

DRAMA is loved by most of humanity and light-workers have to drop it! The drama is related to our karma and once we are out of karma, the drama stops. "Dear Higher Self, dear Spirit, I do not want karma in my life anymore, since it will not serve my purpose of being the light. I want to be the light and give pure intent to drop my karma."

ANGER is most destructive, since by its nature it opposes compassion and love. Unfortunately, there will always be people or events that create energies that have the potential to make us angry, if we allow it. It is about how we react to the things that trigger the anger. It is like a button that somebody presses and we get angry – or not. This will help: "Dear Spirit, dear Higher Self, I do not want anger in my life and when anything presses my anger buttons, I don't want them to work anymore."

FEAR is an emotional program, ingrained into our consciousness or sub-consciousness, which makes us react to the uncertainty of tomorrow. All fear is based on a future aspect, something that might or might not happen. We don't fear the events from the past that led to today, instead we project some bad experience of the past into the future or now – and usually think the worst of it.

There is also a special fear in the light-worker, the fear of everything that has to do with enlightenment, because in the past it did not go well many times. It was about surviving spirituality, always fighting the dark. But the energies have changed and now you can let go of that fear.

The human reason for fear is obvious, for we cannot foresee the future. So, we don't know. And since we don't know, we assume the worst and this will change so very much! If you have a team on the other side, one that knows about the potentials of things to happen and even arranges the synchronicities for you, such as meeting the right people who will help you, at the right time, then there is no room for fear! You are not alone; you are dearly loved and always guided!

Without drama, anger and fear you can plant and water the seeds of light with your own light.

HEAL YOURSELF

This is one of the most powerful tools, the principle of spontaneous remission put onto you, which is the full activation of the DNA even for a short period of time.

With the increasing energy on Earth, DNA-activation and consciousness levels of humans, we can bring forward pure health from earlier lifetimes, when we also lived longer.

We can grow slowly into it through the division of our cells in the body. Every time new cells are produced, they run the new updated healthy program. "Dear cellular structure, dear Spirit, dear DNA, bring forward health, youth and what I need to have."

Envision yourself as healed, create in your mind a strong picture of your healed self, for your innate will recognize the intent and react to it very quickly. A good daily affirmation would be: "I am healthy! There is no sickness, no pain and no disease in my body. My skin is youthful and radiant, my bones are strong and in alignment, my body is strong and flexible. I have the ideal height-weight ratio. All my chakras are in balance."

BELIEVE AND TRUST

You need to believe in the workings of synchronicity until you depend on them and know how to work them. Synchronicity requires that you are in sync with yourself.

The veil to the other side is a dimensional barrier and that barrier moves with belief. It's a belief that grows with experience of Spirit, a knowing. This is your mindset to make anything happen: "I believe and trust in the synchronicity of Spirit and my own creative power!"

SLOW DOWN GETTING OLD

This is the dream of humanity and we need a mixed approach of science and Spirit to solve this riddle. Currently, most of us think 100 years is a long lifespan for a human life. The energy presently supports an age of up to 300 years, but it takes a combination of factors to reach that, namely the combination of science and Spirit!

Spiritual tools: "Dear Spirit, dear cellular structure, use the original blueprint when making new cells. Lengthen the Telomeres!" This can help solve the problems with the shortening of Telomeres, for the new cells also have longer Telomeres. A telomere is a region of repetitive nucleotide sequences at each end of a chromosome, which protects the end of the chromosome from deterioration. Every time the chromosome divides, the telomere becomes shorter.

Template affirmation: "Dear Innate, activate the Genesis Template and activate the Youthing Template."

General affirmation: "Dear DNA, dear Spirit, dear cellular structure, slow down getting old and bring forward youth and health!"

Scientific tools: In order to slow down getting old and to maintain a healthy body, we need moderate exercises with good breathing, like Yoga. Furthermore, a balanced diet with healthy, fresh food and drink is essential.

Recent studies have shown that the aging of cells occurs in several ways, largely because of our modern lifestyles. The result is that there is not enough building material to make new and healthy RNA and DNA.

Some studies showed the enhancement of cells on a molecular level by using light pulses and the injecting of a solution of RNA and DNA into mature mammals (rats). The worst score was double the lifespan of the mammal, and the best triple the lifespan.

There are two major aging clocks in the body, according to the leading scientist in the field. One chemical marker of aging is the level of Homocysteine in the blood, while the other one is the shortening of the Telomeres. There already are products on the market to address these issues and time will show their efficacy.

After using CELLFOOD, a DNA-regenerating formula by the Nu Science Corporation in U.S.A., in a three-month trial, the Homocysteine levels in my blood were lowered by one point, which is quite remarkable.

There is also scientific proof that a positive and happy attitude towards life keeps the body younger. (Dr. Bruce Lipton, Book: The Power of Belief, YouTube: The Biology of Belief, https://youtu.be/jjj0xVM4x1I)

Be the light and see the light in others first!

HOW TO TALK TO THE SPIRIT

Ask for the Spirit to repeat the intuitive thought and the concepts and gradually develop intuitive reception. If you have no idea what it is all about and how it works, ask this: "God, please tell me what I need to know". You don't need to specify what you want! Then Spirit can also access the Akash and bring forward qualities from past lives into now. You don't need to understand how the engine works to drive a car.

ATTITUDE FOR NOW

Optimism, because we know what is happening and nothing can stop the energy.

Celebration, because we are past the doom of prediction and can see the seed of light.

Joy, because the more we activate our connection the more our cells vibrate in joy.

Laughter, because that energy shatters old energy patterns.

These attitudes should be applied, despite what you see in the daily news! Remember, the news is the advertising channel of the dark energy to keep you in a state of fear. With fear in your heart there is no light! You are holding the master key to your destiny.

UNEXPECTED BENEVOLENT CHANGE

Old souls receive a bonus within this new energy, because they carry and move more light and their decisions carry more weight. This is the new formula of what to expect: unexpected benevolent change!

GAIA AND THE ANCESTORS

In order to harness all the energies available, one has to connect to Gaia, maybe even talk to her on a regular basis. Gaia is the consciousness of the planet, interwoven with humanity in a multi-dimensional way through the grids. Use grounding and rooting exercises, as explained later in the book, to connect better and thank Gaia for the support.

Better still, honor Gaia on a daily basis. "Dear Gaia, I love you! Thank you for all the love and help and for the new energy on the planet."

The ancestors play an important role in the multi-dimensional fabric, for they represent the wisdom of the ancients. Furthermore, as an old soul you are your own ancestors. This also should be honored on a daily basis. "Dear ancestors, I love you! Thank you for all the love and wisdom!"

LOVE YOURSELF

Look into the mirror and love yourself! This is not meant in an egotistical, conceited way, but to love the Divine part within. It will create the entanglement of the cells and the innate body recognizes the intuitive thought.

Look into the mirror and say: "I love you! You are doing a great job!" If you don't mean it, the body knows. The cells know the truth, you can't lie and it is recognized when the affirmation is pure. This is an important step to gain DNA-activation, for it is not able to kick in if you don't love yourself. Loving yourself creates a pathway for the cells to listen.

Do you have problems with loving yourself? Remember, in truth you are an eternal piece of the Creator. You are here by your own agreement to work the puzzle of light and dark, without knowing much of it at birth, when you attach yourself to this body. Is that not worth loving yourself? Isn't that deserving of that love?

CELLS ARE LISTENING

Repetition does not work! It is not an old energy linear process. Since birth, the cells have been waiting for you to awaken to the new way of communication. They are part of you and understand your language, you don't have to use codes or symbols. You can think, speak or write to your cells and it will be recognized, because the cells are always listening.

The key is LOVE, love to the cellular structure. Health, healing and youthfulness come with the division of cells, for the new information is used when the cycles refresh over time.

This kick-starts automatic systems that begin improving other parts of the body that you did not ask for, which will also extend our bodies' lifespan.

THE NINE INVOCATIONS
AND AFFIRMATIONS

GAIA: (Multi-dimensional part of the planet) "Honor to Gaia, I love you. Thanks for all the love, support and the new energy of the planet."

ANCESTORS: "Honor to the Ancestors, I love you. Thanks for all the wisdom and love."

HIGHER SELF: (Soul part in 3-D) "Dear Higher Self, I love you. I want a complete meld with my consciousness. Please help me in all things, especially to be more light. I am out of karma, drama, anger, fear, life lessons and vows. Help me to touch the Creator inside."

INNATE: (Part of Higher Self, but separate) "Dear Innate, I love you. Good job! I want a complete meld with my consciousness. I am a master, a healer, a teacher and a Yogi. I am an artist and a scientist. I am love, compassion and joy. I am light and I attract light. Bring forward from my Akash what I need to have now and hold back that which does not serve my purpose as a piece of the Creator. I am healthy, I am wealthy and I am in abundance of all things. Great things are coming my way. Today is a great day! Today I have solutions for my problems. There is no pain, sickness or disease in my body, there is nothing in my body that does not reflect my magnificence. I have the ideal height-weight ratio. My bones are strong and in alignment, my body is strong and flexible, and my skin is youthful and radiant. I am not getting older today, I am youthing. My life span is 300 years. I can see energies and I can manifest. I am in control of my life and my desires. Whatever I create is in highest demand! Dear Innate, activate the DNA fully and increase the vibration of all cells. When making new cells, go to the original blueprint. Lengthen the Telomeres. Activate the Genesis template and activate the Youthing template. All my chakras are in balance."

GUIDES: (Part of Higher Self) "Dear guides, I love you. Thank you for all the guidance and love. Please speak up, repeat and slow down the guidance until I do understand."

ANGELS: "Dear angels, I love you. Thank you for all the light and love. Please pour your light over me always."

SPIRITUAL ENTOURAGE: (Part of Higher Self, part others, e.g., family and friends who passed on) "Dear entourage, I love you. Thank you for the love and for creating the synchronicities that I meet the right people at the right place and time, who have solutions to my problems, as I have for them, too."

BEINGS OF LIGHT: (Our lineage from the stars) "Dear beings of light, thanks for attaching to me and increasing my vibration." (The cells are not really vibrating higher in 3-D, they become more multi-dimensional.)

SOUL: (Soul part in Multi-D) "Dear soul, I love you."

"Dear Spirit, please put me where you need me, where I can be the most light to others. Thank you, Spirit, for creating the abundance, I love it! Please give me more! I believe in miracles in my life! Glory to the Creator, for I am a magnificent piece of God! I am that I am, I am."

Look into your eyes in the mirror and say : "I love you"

This teaching is the most powerful set of instructions for light workers until 2030, when it will be replaced by non-linear teaching. Love and light.

PHYSICS OF THE NEW AGE

Presently, humans use four laws of physics and have a limited understanding of nature, since there are two laws missing that soon will be discovered and will enable us to formulate a complete unified theory of physics:

Strong electro-magnetic force (Gravity)

Weak electro-magnetic force (Electro-Magnetism)

Strong nuclear force (Strong Nuclear Force)

Weak nuclear force (Weak Nuclear Force)

Strong multi-dimensional force (NEW)

Weak multi-dimensional force (NEW)

When finally discovered and understood, this new theory will also explain dark matter and dark energy – which are invisible in 3-D.

TEN SPIRITUAL TRUTHS

1. We are multi-dimensional beings working the puzzle of light on Earth.

2. Our essence is eternal.

3. All is vibration.

4. Thoughts create reality because energy follows thought.

5. On Earth we have free will to go towards light or dark.

6. Old souls incarnated on this planet for 1,000 + lifetimes.

7. We are never alone and are always supported.

8. Time is an illusion of the 4-dimensional universe.

9. We passed Armageddon in 2,000 and the maker of the test in 2012.

10. Love, compassion and joy are the greatest powers of the New Age.

Men using religion, doctrine or dogma to suppress, intimidate or abuse women are a relic of the energetic past and will eventually fade out of this planet in one or the other way – it is time for men to understand that the intuitive power of women is much stronger, they are simply more connected to the Creative Source.

Your intent is the catalyst for the consciousness shift available to you. The biggest part of you is not in 3-D, since only a small part of the soul can live in a human being that has activated just about 30 percent of its DNA. Connecting to this non-3-D part of you is the task, since it will open the door to everything.

Thanks to my friends and enemies who have agreed to interact with me in this lifetime, to provide the lessons needed!

PORTALS

It is good to allocate one place for spiritual routine. Prayer, meditation and healing over time create a multi-dimensional gate at that location, which stays forever!

Anybody sensitive enough to feel it and know what to do, can access it. Most will say: "Oh, what a nice place you have, it feels so good". Few will see the whole multi-dimensional process of the portal, and find healing and more.

How big and strong the portal is, depends on YOU and everyone who helps you to grow it. Since there is strength in numbers, a portal really 'kicks in' after several group events. The more a portal is used, the more energy it can hold - there is no limit to that.

AFTERLIFE

Let's talk about eternity. Most Christians believe that after this life they will either go to an eternal heaven or hell. It is much harder for the same people to understand that eternity, the time-less condition 'on the other side', includes the past as well.

We are eternal beings in both directions, there is no beginning and no end! There is a plan though, and it is not to 'go to heaven, sing and play the harp' for all eternity. God's plan is much grander and efficient.

Maybe you should think about what you did before this lifetime, and before - and before the first one on Earth. Remember, you are eternal! You worked the light on many planets, galaxies and even universes.

Eternal means ALWAYS and FOREVER.

That is what you truly are, an eternal piece of God, even if you don't remember! This is the puzzle. Be the example of a compassionate God and let that shape your future.

Is there a heaven and hell? There is no such thing as heaven or hell. It's a man-made strategy to control human beings. There is only home! Heaven and hell are on this planet, depending what you make of your life, and the only justice is the karma that humans bring into this lifetime. This explains why we are not equal and why some seem to have more fortunate lives than others. We are not all the same, we are different because of our past! Only when we are back home in multi-dimensionality are we equal pieces of the Creator.

Part 2:

The Esoteric of the New Age
and Healing Techniques for Healers

HOW DOES HEALING WORK

All healing is SELF-HEALING. A healer can create a multi-dimensional higher vibrating portal to accelerate the self-healing process, though.

The combined factors to achieve a great self-healing are: belief and platform.

Belief:

The more a human believes in and expects healing, the better it will work. The scientific proof is the placebo effect, a remarkable phenomenon in which a placebo – a fake treatment, an inactive substance like sugar, distilled water, or saline solution – can sometimes improve a patient's condition simply because the person has the expectation that it will be helpful.

Many medical doctors have witnessed a process called 'instantaneous remission', when a terminally sick patient unexpectedly gets well within hours or days and there is no explanation for it.

There are references in the Bible about the great Master Healer Jesus who taught a lame man this same principle: "It was your belief that healed you."

The fact that one can find abandoned crutches in churches of many faiths and religions is proof that healing is not limited to one doctrine or faith.

Platform:

For self-healing capabilities to kick in, a multi-dimensional energetic platform has to be provided, something that vibrates at a higher rate than the patient. Scientists have recently found that healing happens when the brain enters a gamma state and the heart centre is activated.

Most energy healers and shamans can easily do this, as well as most New Age professionals. Miracle crusade healers also operate in such a way, which creates a valid platform for miracles through the power of belief of the masses. Healing is always supported by the collective consciousness of a large group of people with a similar mindset.

Healing can also be achieved by daily affirmation, prayer, meditation, yoga, dance, exercise, trance, magic, herbs, medicines and drugs, and by many other unique means, which are designed to work with that specific human, like a change of habit or diet.

Finally, healing is supported at special places in nature and even in man-made structures, designs and machines. Healing is self-healing, it is YOU with YOU, mind over body – consciousness over matter.

PRE-CONDITION OF HEALING

As a healer, be healthy! Nobody wants to go to a healer who is riddled with ailments. Use daily affirmations such as the following: "I am healthy", "I have the ideal body height-weight ratio", "I am strong and flexible", "My spine is in alignment", "There is nothing in my body that does not serve my magnificence", etc.

The potential of healing depends on pure INTENT and strong BELIEF in the process by both the healer and the patient.

PREPARATION OF THE HEALING PLACE

Keep in mind that your workplace is holy and therefore has to be clean. If you are lucky enough to use an outside area, spraying plants, earth and stones with water will de-ionize the air and guarantee a great smell of wet earth and fresh plants.

When using incense, make sure there is good airflow in the room/area. Sandalwood is a very pleasing and uplifting smell, and Frankincense is a great cleanser and works with the crown chakra.

Large, clean crystals in all colors and shapes are beautiful for decorating the place, increasing its vibration and helpful for healing. Use meditative, chanting music to create a lovely ambience and to cover up the mundane neighborhood noises. Listen to your intuition when acquiring crystals, incense and music, and the right ones will come to you.

Make sure the healing process is comfortable to you and the patient, and that you will not be disturbed!

THE BREATHING

The right breathing is essential for success and the strongest technique is called Ujjayi in Sanskrit, which translates into 'victorious breath'. It has been used in meditation for ages to connect to the light and the Yogis are very familiar with it.

The best way to describe Ujjayi is to imagine breathing through a hose-pipe (energetic tube) that runs along the spine from the tailbone to the top of your head. To be more specific, it's from the location of the root chakra between genitals and anus to crown chakra at the fusing point of the frontal fontanel.

With the slow and deep inhale, pull the energy from Earth via the root chakra through your body up into the crown chakra. Hold the breath for two seconds and exhale. With the slow and deep exhale, pull the energy from heaven via the crown chakra through the body into the hands and then down to root. Hold the breath again before the next inhale. (Do not hold your breath when pregnant!)

To further strengthen the energy flow, with the inhale, think of the energy in your spine as a rotating tube, pull your bottom Bandhas (muscles in pelvic floor) and with the exhale draw the belly towards the spine. This very slow and deep Ujjayi breathing is the norm during the light healing and is Yin-orientated. Occasionally though, we can use stronger breathing, more Yang-related, pushing focused faster breaths with the exhaling into our hands.

For the upcoming higher light breathing techniques you need to be easy, relaxed and comfortable in deep Ujjayi breathing!

THE MINDSET

To make healing really happen, it would not be enough just to ask for healing and help from the universe, but rather repeating: "It's already done – it's already healed – thank you, God." In our mindset, the sickness and the successful healing are in the past.

We are creating a new and healthy future. The more the patient believes in the healer and the process, the stronger the possibility of instantaneous healing.

CHAKRAS

The chakras are small, colorful balls of energy, and the human's main receptors and transformers of the bright Divine white light into the denser physical level. Here is a list of the major 7 chakras.

The split of the Divine white light into the light of the lower vibrating colors is obvious.

Crown:

Location:	Top of head, at fusing point of the frontal fontanel, opening upwards.
Color:	Violet
Mantra:	AUM
Function:	Higher Dimensions
Action:	Communication with Divine

Affirmation: "I am one with all that is. I choose to live my life from a place of love and contentment. I am connected to the Higher Power. I create my reality."

Third-eye:

Location:	Centre of the brow and back of the head.
Color:	Deep blue (indigo)
Mantra:	OM
Function:	Spiritual Balance
Action:	Awakening Intuition

Affirmation: "I recognize the need for silence and stillness in my life. I trust my vision, my intuition and my feelings. I am full of wisdom and intelligence. I am able to discern for my greatest good."

Throat:

Location: Between lower throat and back of the neck.

Color: Light blue (turquoise)

Mantra: HAM

Function: Expression

Action: Solutions

Affirmation: "I honestly express my thoughts, feelings and ideas with grace. I release gossip, lies and addictions that no longer serve me from my life. I listen to myself and I trust my inner voice."

Heart:

Location: Centre of the chest on the sternum and back.

Color: Green and pink

Mantra: YAM

Function: Relationships

Action: Connecting

Affirmation: "I am open to give and receive love. Love connects me to all that is. Love will set me free."

Solar plexus:

Location: Centre of solar plexus at bottom of the sternum and middle back.

Color: Yellow

Mantra: RAM

Function: DNA repair

Action: Transformation and miracles

Affirmation: "I am open to receive all good things in life. I am the only one who has the power to approve of me. I can achieve anything that I desire. I am confident and strong."

Sacral:

Location: Two-finger width below navel and above sacrum.

Color: Orange

Mantra: VAM

Function: Facilitating change

Action: Undoing situations

Affirmation: "I am connected to my inner source of inspiration. I honor my physical body temple. I have joyful and harmonious relationships. Life is unfolding as it is supposed to."

Root:

Location: Between anus and genitals and opening downwards.

Color: Red

Mantra: LAM

Function: Grounding

Action: Liberating guilt and fear

Affirmation: "I am taking responsibility for my life and I can cope with any situation. All my needs are met. I am one with all of life."

To uplift the body's vibration, the chakras have to be energized with light. After several sessions, the whole body will remain at a higher energy level, and one will remain more uplifted.

The chakras are the energetic backbone of the human through all layers of aura (the field that is around the physical body), transforming energy from the highest level down to the physical level.

When a patient comes with great pain in his body, it might be the best to first heal the etheric body and relieve the pain first. That might also give permanent relief, if the pain is acute and related to injury.

In cases of prolonged suffering over time such as with chronic disease, we face a much more complicated situation, for there are strong imprints in the higher levels of the aura. Within guidance, use your spiritual logic!

THE LAYERS OF THE AURA

Most of the older emotional baggage has an imprint in the higher layers of the aura.

The seven layers of the aura are:

> Etheric body
>
> Emotional layer
>
> Mental layer
>
> Astral layer
>
> Etheric template
>
> Celestial body
>
> Spiritual or causal layer

The first three layers are an indication of the physical, emotional and mental experience of the physical body; the fourth layer is the bridge and the last three layers do represent physical, emotional and mental experiences in the spiritual world. Since personality is the combination of distinctive characteristics or qualities, it will essentially be the total sum of the energies of ALL layers that make one's personality. With an average person, the auras can be felt from 1 cm for the etheric layer up to 1 meter for the causal layer. Problems that are within the layers are often indicated if the colors of an aura appear dull, muddy or darkened rather than bright.

The first layer, the etheric body, is the densest layer with the lowest vibration. It is the layer, closest to the physical body and reflects the condition of the physical body. The etheric body consists of Ether, the lowest vibrating multi-dimensional energy in 4-D, a sparkling web of light which is bound in structure to the physical shape of the living organism. This is the physical level of the physical body. The dominant color of this layer seems to be shades of blue.

The second layer of the aura is the field that holds emotions and feelings. In this layer are our senses of sight, sound, taste, smell and touch – as well as our intuition, our 'sixth sense'. This is the emotional level of the physical body. The colors usually fluctuate within the rainbow spectrum, according to the emotions.

The third layer contains the structure of ideas, thoughts and mental processes. This is the mental level of the physical body. The colors are bright shades of yellow, which indicate a clear thinking process and a sense of purpose. Yellow is known to greatly enhance the thinking process.

The fourth layer, the astral layer, represents the bridge between the physical and spiritual worlds. It is also related to the emotional level and to higher emotions, like compassion and empathy (unconditional love). Also, within this layer negative emotions such as fear and anger are processed. The colors are within the spectrum of a rainbow, but usually tend to be green.

The fifth layer contains a blueprint of all the forms of the physical world, including the master copy for the etheric layer to model the physical body. This is the physical level of the spiritual plane. The colors can vary.

The sixth layer is our connection to the spiritual realm; all communication moves via this layer. This is the emotional level of the spiritual plane, and is characterized by a great feeling of unconditional love and joy. Its colors are pastel colors.

The seventh layer (spiritual or causal) extends the furthest from the physical body and is the highest vibrating level. This level is our protection and where life experience is kept; it is the level where we meld with the consciousness of the Creator. This is the mental level of the spiritual plane. The color is gold.

PREPARATION

The purpose of preparation is to bring your energy levels into a higher state, for the human to give time to step aside and let the Spirit enter the consciousness. Preparation was always needed in the past until 2012, since the darkness was pushing at us.

Since the shift of the energy, especially from 2014, there is a new scenario for the healer. If the healer is melding with the Innate and Higher Self and has become the Divine white light, there is no 'switch on – switch off' anymore – the Divine white light is always on. No ritual, no cleansing and no preparation is needed, the healer is always ready and protected!

There is a simple step from old energy healer to 'New Age' healer. The expression 'New Age' has been misused a lot, but a new age it is nevertheless. We passed the energetic marker of 2012 and new tools are now available as we develop.

It has always been the basic understanding that the energy healer is technically a channel of universal energy, called chi, life force and so forth. This was the reality of the healer of the old energy before the energetic shift of the planet.

In the new energy of now, there is a new healer emerging, one that has the understanding, that behind the universal energy is the Divine white light, pure energy of the Creator. When 'switching on' the Divine white light inside and understanding that one is a piece of God, the healer becomes the source of the Divine white light. Whilst shining bright, the healer continues to channel, but on a different level. The healer is one with the process at all levels.

The bridge to the Divine has never been wider; here is how to cross it as fast as possible:

Recognition of the Divine white light.

Wanting to meld with the Divine white light, whilst healing others and working as a channel of light.

Becoming the Divine white light.

This comes hand-in-hand with the healer's most powerful tool, namely: Compassionate action. Remember, there is no 'selective' compassion!

ROOTING

A valid preparation that puts you into the energetic middle of your existence is the rooting exercise, which puts you between heaven and Earth right in the center.

The rooting exercise is also very effective for patients before healing:

Breathe deeply and in a relaxed fashion. After three breaths, imagine a massive root drilling from each foot right into the core of Earth. Take three breaths to imagine that.

Then imagine many, many smaller roots drilling from each foot down; they do not extent very deeply, but there are plenty of them. Again, take three breaths to imagine that.

Take all the time you need to pull the energy of Gaia through your roots with the inhale, up through your body above your crown chakra. With the exhale, draw the energy back from heaven to Earth.

Tip: Start the day with this affirmation: "Honor to Gaia. I love you. Thank you for all the love and support and thank you for the new energy on the planet."

GOLDEN EGG OF LIGHT

This visualization is a well-known and very powerful protection!

With a deep inhale, imagine a golden egg of light around you, protecting you from any negativity from the outside.

Repeat this visualization three times.

STARBURST TECHNIQUE

I have developed the Starburst technique for its great potential to increase the light within. Most people have seen an animation of a 'Supernova' or the explosion of a star on TV or the Internet. The Starburst technique is just that! Imagine igniting the Starburst right from the middle of your heart and letting the light ripple through all your layers of aura and existence.

With a deep inhale fill up your body with pure light, hold your breath for a short moment and ignite the Starburst. When exhaling, feel the light ripple through you towards the outside. Repeat this three times. This will greatly enhance your ability to radiate more light and is also a great way to protect against negative energy!

THE MASTER HEALING PRINCIPLE

When inhaling, honor Gaia and pull the energies of Gaia through the feet and your body up, draw attention upwards and reach through the crown chakra to the Divine white light while thinking "Glory to God – for I am a magnificent part of God".

With the exhale, draw the light into the hands while thinking "Glory to the Divine Mother" or any mantra praising God, or any holy entity according to your religion and preference. The above-mentioned mantra also harmonizes the male and female aspect of the Creator.

This technique is now the basic one for every inhale and exhale of breath. Essentially you are glorifying God with each breath – with the realization of being a piece of God, which is why it is so powerful.

The final addition to the flow of energy is your part as Co-Creator that allows you to pour love, compassion and joy into the healing and to use your knowledge, wisdom and spiritual logic.

During the healing, ask your team of angels, guides and Spirits to pour as much light into you as you can hold and handle safely, then shine your inner Divine white light bright, by activating the Starburst.

WRAPPING IN SILVER, GOLD AND LIGHT

Visualize the patient wrapped in layers of silver, gold and pure Divine white light from head to feet and back. This can be done several times during the ongoing treatment.

Refresh the memory of its brilliant shine of silver and gold, by looking at objects of the pure metals like rings, jewelry, etc.

LOVE, COMPASSION AND JOY

Before the shift of 2012, the highest energy available for healers was LOVE and it still is the base of most healing methods available. Since the shift, we are able to use the next higher level of compassion, which is generated by the increased consciousness of humanity.

As it happens with love, there are several layers of compassion, starting with the compassion towards one self, then to others and then moving into the final state, which is unconditional compassion. This is based on the realization that there is no difference between others and oneself, since we are all pieces of the Creator who are playing our various parts.

The energetic numeric value of compassion is 33 and corresponds very much with the percentage of DNA activated by most humans at this moment. For most healers in the new energy, the expression of compassion will bring amazing new results and will shorten the time needed for healing sessions.

However, there are exceptions. Very old souls who re-calibrated early and have already moved into the next activation level of 44 percent of DNA, are much more connected to the Source. Because of their close connection to the Source, they also experience the overwhelming joy of it and will be able to reflect that ultimate joy into the healing process.

My prediction of the energetic value of 44 is 'Joy of Creator' and only people with a direct experience of the Creator can use this energy to its fullest in healing. Otherwise, it helps to remember the most joyful thing in your life, capture that feeling and recall it during healing.

This will be the future standard for all humans within a few lifetimes and the norm for healers from the next life.

STANDING CHAKRA TREATMENT

The aim of this exercise is to balance and to raise the vibration of all the patient's chakras and to help the healer to tune in with the breathing, energy flow and Divine white light. This is the final preparation before tuning into even higher vibrations.

Commence with the standing Chakra treatment and ensure that the patient is standing comfortably and feels secure.

Breathing (Master healing principle)

Place left hand on the crown and the other at the lower spine (coccyx) – stay for three breaths.

Place both hands at the exit points of the third-eye chakra and stay for three breaths.

Place both hands at exit points of the throat chakra and stay for three breaths.

Place both hands at exit points of the heart chakra and stay for three breaths.

Place both hands at exit points of the solar plexus chakra and stay for three breaths.

Place both hands at exit points of the sacral chakra and stay for three breaths.

Again, place left hand on the crown and the other on the lower spine (coccyx) – stay for three breaths.

Place both hands at exit points of the sacral chakra and stay for three breaths.

Place both hands at exit points of the solar plexus chakra and stay for three breaths.

Place both hands at exit points of the heart chakra and stay for three breaths.

Place both hands at exit points of the throat chakra and stay for three breaths.

Place both hands at exit points of the third-eye chakra and stay for three breaths.

Finally, place left hand on the crown and the other at the lower spine (coccyx) and stay for three breaths.

THREE-COLOR TECHNIQUE

Breathing (linking praise with Ujjayi Breathing)

With the inhale, focus at the crown and connect to the bright Divine white light. Take only the green portion of the white light and link this radiant green light with the energy of pure love. With the exhale, draw this green light of pure love into your hands and into the patient. Repeat for three breaths.

With the inhale, focus at the crown and connect to the bright Divine white light. Take only the pink portion of the white light and link this radiant pink light with the energy of unconditional love (it is helpful to realize that we are all ONE). With the exhale, draw this pink light of compassion into your hands and into the patient. Repeat for three breaths.

With the inhale, focus at the crown and connect to the bright Divine white light. Take the white light and link this radiant white light with the energy of pure joy. With the exhale, draw this white light of joy into your hands and into the patient. Repeat for three breaths.

SWITCH LOADER TECHNIQUE

This exercise is designed to remove the focus from the process and enable stronger flow of the Divine white light.

The principle of the technique is to move your attention and focus from one hand to the other back and forth in quick sequence. There are several ways of achieving this, e.g., with one hand on the heart chakra and the other on the solar plexus chakra:

Move your eyes from one hand to the other. Left-right, left-right.

Gently press down and lift up your hands, just a tiny bit. Left-right, left-right.

Move mentally from one hand to the other. Left-right, left-right.

Repeat for three breaths. Now every time when focusing on one hand, create a spark from this hand to the other and vice versa until the Divine white light between the hands is connected and there is a strong energy pull.

Let go of the focus of the hands and with the inhale set your focus at the crown into the bright Divine white light, and stay there with your focus and let the Divine white light flow freely!

If the flow of Divine white light is not sustainable, repeat the whole Switch Loader until you are satisfied.

EDGE TECHNIQUE

This is a most advanced Hands-On healing technique with incredible results and has evolved from the Switch Loader Technique. Bring your awareness to the edge of the energy flow between your hands. By moving the hands gently up and down (cat paws), you will feel the pressure of the edge (of the energy) increase and decrease with every move. Therefore, you are able to push and pull the edge of the energy field through the tissue of the patient.

It's easier to feel the edge effect with the inside of the hands towards each other, but it also works well with the hands next to each other. Imagine gently pressing and releasing a balloon in between your hands; when pushing the one side, the pressure on the other hand will increase and vice versa.

HANDS-OFF TECHNIQUE

This technique makes it easier to understand the before-mentioned edge effect and it is simple to guide the energy field between the hands and patient by rotating, pushing and pulling the hands. Awareness should be towards the energy field, its edge and the switch of polarization, where the magnetic plus becomes minus and vice versa, when moving the hands.

When pushing the hands together or towards the patient, the pressure seems to increase. When pulling back one can observe the delay, like suction. Furthermore, by adding a rotation to the push-and-pull movement of the hands, the energy can be easily guided to flood the patient more efficiently. It is not a coincidence that this looks very similar to the conductor of an orchestra; but instead of musicians we are guiding energies. The distance of the hands to the body is variable, depending on your preference and aim.

HIPULSE TECHNIQUE

The HiPulse is the most advanced technique so far and derives its name from the high pulsations of the magnetic healing field that is generated. Start the technique by moving the hands in slow circular motions towards each other, pointing towards the patient. After you get comfortable with the movement of the energy, you can double the speed of the motion at several stages, as long as you feel comfortable and keep a 'grip' on the energy.

This technique is physically taxing, for it puts strain on shoulders and arms, so make sure to shake loose your hands and arms from time to time. The fastest move can be assimilated through the shaking of the hands, which is not as exhausting as moving the arms the whole time.

After some time using this technique and programming the reality of it into your system, you can finally try to envision the technique mentally and speed up even faster. The energy provided grows incrementally with the speed used to move the energy field.

HEALING IN A NUTSHELL

Generation of energy

Since using only human life force for healing would result in a quick depletion of the energy, healing systems use the unlimited supply of energy around us. Most healing systems are teaching ways to increase the flow of energy, usually by increasing the vibration of the healer, and using mental bridges to load a higher vibration into the consciousness. This can be done with colors, music, mantras and geometrical shapes, for instance. Some healing modalities use mental techniques to increase the vibration of the patient as well.

All the many healing systems or modalities available today have one thing in common, namely the transformation of energy.

Transformation of energy

Transformation of energy is also the sole difference between the healing systems, or the way or formula of how to generate and transfer the energy. Before explaining the technical aspects of healing, I would like to remind you of the essential pre-condition necessary for a healer: purity and sincerity of the heart.

The most common way of healing is by using the hands, where the energy is distributed via the chakra inside of the hand and the tips of the fingers. Some healing systems apply touch to the patient, whereas others do not. Both have their advantages and any serious healer should know and apply both. Since most people are deprived of loving touch, it is usually beneficial to employ touch. Distance is needed if it is not advisable to touch (if the patient is contagious, there are open or burn wounds, etc.); if it is improper (root chakra, code of ethics, religion); if it is impossible (distance healing to a different location); or if it is desirable (working with the higher layers of the aura).

Another way of healing would be to use the eyes, where the energy is distributed via the chakra in the eyes and last, but not least, there is also a purely mental way of healing, where the energy is distributed via the crown chakra. The most commonly known example would be healing prayer or some ways of distance healing. Finally, the master oozes the Divine white light as a whole; it is not limited to certain exit portals of the body. Some masters have such a powerful light that they can heal by their mere presence.

Healing energy can be transformed without delay in time and space, since in the dimension of the Divine white light, time and space do not exist! The best way of understanding this is to arrange healing sessions using Skype, which will provide instant feedback, despite the distance.

ATTACHING THE MIND AND LETTING GO

Most healing systems attach the mind to the healing process. Healers are usually advised to focus on something, as mentioned earlier at the Generation of Energy chapter. Other modalities detach the mind and just let go and flow.

Until one is very experienced and strong, I would recommend starting healing with attachment of mind and only later when one is vibrating higher, should one detach the mind from the process. Essentially, the healer is like a water pipe. The larger the diameter of the pipe, the more water can flow. The closer we are to the Source of the Divine white light the more energy will be poured into the healer by angels and guides. Even a child can understand this and everybody with a higher vibration can witness it.

To enlarge the diameter of the pipe or to get closer to the Source, we have to link our consciousness to the right breathing and the described exercises. Furthermore, over time we have to grow our faith in the process.

Once we are in the Divine white light, we have to let go! We shouldn't focus on anything else, but only stay connected to the Divine white light, and finally become the Divine white light! Remember, our job is to try to be a vessel for unlimited energy flow, which is a prerequisite for miracles, as is unlimited faith.

There is no need to worry about the healing as such, since it will be done by angels and spiritual healers, by the plan of the universe and the innate intelligence of the body of the patient. Listen to your intuition and be open for guidance.

Letting go will be stronger when one is connected to the Divine white light and faith is not limited!

UPLIFTING THE VIBRATION
WITH MEDITATION

Self-awareness is the 3-D part in humans that is fully aware of the multi-dimensional part. You don't need to search anywhere else for the source of illusion.

Wherever you search externally, you cannot find it, because your illusions come from within your mind. Your mind creates the illusion using the feedback from the senses and makes it 'feel so real' that you believe it.

Meditation, or learning to ignore the senses, is the solution.

Only knowledge (gnosis) of spiritual light - not faith prescribed by clergy - offers escape from the earthly dominion. The purpose of meditation is to deepen the awareness of your own reality and thereby to increase your vibration.

The three main foundations of meditation are: Control of body, breath and mind.

There is no such thing as the 'best meditation' routine or technique, since it works differently for each person. It is important to find what works best for yourself, since the way we experience and perceive energy is different. All higher vibrating souls are able to perceive the higher energies in one way or another. Everybody has to develop his/her own abilities of perception.

BREATHING FOR MEDITATION

The right breathing is essential for success and the strongest technique is called Ujjayi in Sanskrit or "Victorious Breath". It has been used in meditation for ages to connect to the light and forms the basis of true Yogis' practice. These Yogis are not to be confused with people doing the movements or Asanas of Yoga in an aerobic-like style, as it is fashion in the West.

The best way to describe Ujjayi is to imagine breathing through a hose-pipe (energetic tube) that runs along the spine from the tailbone to the top of your head. To be more specific, it's from the location of the root chakra between the genitals and anus up to the crown chakra at the fusing point of the frontal fontanel.

With the slow and deep inhale, pull the energy from Earth via the root chakra through your body up into the crown chakra. Hold the breath for two seconds and exhale. With the slow and deep exhale, pull the energy from heaven via crown chakra through the body into the hands and then down to root. Hold the breath again before the next inhale. (Never hold your breath when pregnant!)

To further strengthen the energy flow, with the inhale think of the energy in your spine as a rotating tube and squeeze your root Bandha (muscles of the pelvic floor). Whilst exhaling, draw the belly towards the spine. For effective meditation, you need to be easy, relaxed and comfortable in deep Ujjayi breathing!

MEDITATION

Here are some simple but powerful examples of how to raise awareness and energy levels; all examples are done sitting in easy posture. Keep your back straight and use a pillow to support your back.

Candle meditation

Place a candle one meter in front of you and look into the flame. Keep your breathing normal and relaxed (no Ujjayi breathing). Observe your breathing for a while. The inhale - followed by the exhale. When inhaling, think: "inhale", when exhaling, think: "exhale". Then put your focus on the flame of the candle. When thoughts come up in your mind, bring your attention back onto the breathing and then when the mind is quiet, back to the flame.

From time to time you may close your eyes and lift your gaze up to focus at the third-eye.

Heart meditation

Eyes closed, using Ujjayi breathing. Inhaling slow and deep with focus at top of crown, exhaling slow with focus at heart and chanting the sacred syllable OM into the heart. This meditation is most helpful to implement the understanding of God inside of you.

Chakra meditation (one-by-one)

Eyes closed, using Ujjayi breathing. Inhaling slow and deep with focus at top of crown, exhaling slow with focus at the 6 lower chakras and chanting the sacred syllable OM into the subsequent chakra up and down:

UP: Inhale crown - exhale root (OM); inhale crown - exhale sacral (OM); inhale crown - exhale solar plexus (OM); inhale crown - exhale heart (OM); inhale crown - exhale throat (OM); inhale crown - exhale third-eye (OM).

DOWN: Inhale crown - exhale third-eye (OM); inhale crown - exhale throat (OM); inhale crown - exhale heart (OM); inhale crown - exhale solar plexus (OM); inhale crown - exhale sacral (OM); inhale crown - exhale root (OM).

These should be done in sets of six!

Advanced chakra meditation (all-in-one)

Eyes closed, using Ujjayi breathing. Breathing is deep and slow, both - inhale and exhale.

Focus with the inhale is to visualize an energy flow from the bottom through the root chakra moving up in an energetic 'tube', passing all the chakras and exiting through the crown chakra.

Focus with the exhale is to visualize an energy flow from the top through the crown chakra moving down in an energetic 'tube', passing all the chakras and exiting through the root chakra. The energy flow is strengthened by chanting the sacred syllable OM with the exhale.

Keep 'monitoring' the process from your space behind the third-eye in a detached way.

Turbo charged chakra meditation (fast breath)

Eyes closed. Just like the one-by-one meditation, only breathing is very fast. Breathing in and out together around two seconds only! Should be done in sets of six!

Easy with this one, increase repetitions only slowly over time and monitor the side effects!

SIDE EFFECTS OF ENERGY WORK

Through the momentary extreme influx of universal Divine white light, spiritual realizations that took years in the past are now achievable in no time. So if you are doing a lot of energy work you will attain a lot for yourself and the universe.

Unfortunately for us though, our bodies are not used to such an enormous energy intake and will therefore suffer. Working with energy has reactions and implications. The following list is by no means complete. More documentation is to be found online:

Extreme heat from the hands and feet, later heat from the whole body

Feeling of flames over the skin

Fever of unknown origin

Flu symptoms

Pain in heart area, heart problems, arrhythmic or too fast

Headache, mild or strong

Neck- and shoulder pain

Pressure at the forehead, between eyebrows or inside the skull

Feeling of a whirling vortex inside the head

Pain in the solar plexus area, vomiting

Diarrhea and other digestive problems

Unexpected weight gain or loss

Unexpected hunger or feeling of starvation

More sensitive to acid in the mouth

More sensitive to noise and light

Problems with eyesight

Skin itches

Numb feeling in face or body parts

Hearing of noises or voices

Seeing of faces, scenes, colors, lights, shapes, angels or Spirits

Memory problems

Feeling of loss of identity

Interference with electrical and electronic devices

Detachment from reality

Usually the head-related symptoms will fade out when the third-eye chakra has opened. Let's embrace everything with the smiling understanding that it is all for the best and part of the grander plan. Besides, we are all here by our own choice and plan. It takes a lot of heat and pressure to create a diamond!

HEALING TOOLS FOR THE NEW AGE

An increased vibration presents us with unprecedented tools for light-workers. It is important to understand the correlation of the Divine white light and our genetics. Science calls it the DNA phantom effect, how DNA and light interact on a quantum level (Vladimir Poponin, 1992: *The DNA Phantom Effect: Direct Measurement of a New Field in the Vacuum Substructure*).

The DNA of every cell of your body is in a quantum state of connectedness, all-knowing. It is on this root level that we are one with the universe – the seat of the soul in 3-D is spread into every cell – located in the 90 percent random part of DNA, scientists called the "junk-DNA".

With the right insight and intent, we can communicate with the DNA and tell it to set free our best potentials for this lifetime in health, wisdom or any attribute and to vibrate higher. That way we are becoming more quantum, as a whole. We can re-program the DNA with pure mind! The quantum field of your DNA includes all possibilities; you only have to tell it what you want!

"Dear Spirit, dear DNA, dear cellular 'quantumness' that is in me, examine my life and give me those things which will enhance it." This is the general invocation, but you can also ask for specific attributes like health, strength, wisdom and youth.

This is a new way of healing yourself or your patients on a quantum level and is strongly supported by giving Divine white light healing. Again, the Divine white light touches at quantum level and is even able to remove genetic markers and disease. Once the DNA is re-programmed, it will continue to produce only healthy cells and over a short period of time one outgrows disease.

FINAL THOUGHTS

This has been an insight into my healing techniques and teachings. Take from it what resonates with you and discard that which does not. We are all different and unique.

When my personal journey of awakening happened and I was ready to answer my call as healer and teacher, I had Divine visions, experiences and synchronicities and thought this was special, only to realize later that it's a new normal.

A good path to reaching a high level of vibration quickly is to exchange healing sessions with other healers on a regular base, to meditate and to be the reflection of a compassionate God.

The Divine Creator is right inside of your every single cell, you are a part of God!

Switch on your inner Divine white light and walk life as a radiant piece of the Creator and remember that, no matter what comes your way, you have an unlimited supply of Divine white light – you can never be depleted! You are the Light and darkness cannot attack you!

Welcome to the new "New Age" of light and information, OM Shanti; Lokah Samastah Sukhino Bhavantu (*Sanskrit for: The peace of the God; may all beings be happy and free and may my own thoughts, words and actions contribute to the happiness and freedom of all*), love and light.

Glory to the Creator, for I am a magnificent piece of God!

This manual is based on insights and input from many humans of great thought and wisdom, some ancient and some recent.

In 1991 I read "Autobiography of a Yogi" by Paramahansa Yogananda and in the following year I was initiated into Kriya Yoga. Some 24 years later I experienced several visions and my first complete connection to the Source. Some of the insights I have received, and still receive, are included in this book.

A lot of the information in this book is inspired by the teachings of KRYON, master of magnetism, a loving helping angelic entity or group, originally channeled by Lee Carroll. If you like this book, you will love Kryon! For more information please visit: www.kryon.com.

The purpose of this manual is to get you out of any box you might be in, and with better understanding you will achieve a better connection and awareness of the process of using the universal energy. With more awareness comes the ability to work with higher levels of light frequencies that are new and available. Eventually the phrase "I want to be the light" will become "I am the light," and that is ascension-level mastery.

Understanding and practicing this truth for a short while will have substantial increase in the ability to hold more light, which will reflect itself in more heat emanating from the hands and body of a light-worker. Your light will shine permanently!

Please contact me for any questions, comments or recommendations. Love and light.